I Ca
Find It!

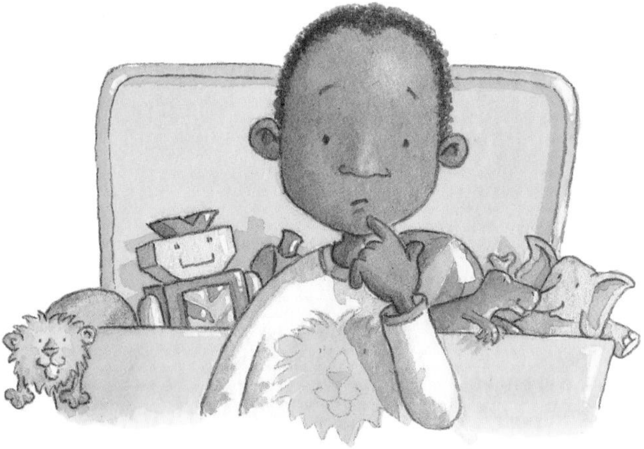

Jill Atkins

Illustrated by Sami Sweeten

RIGBY

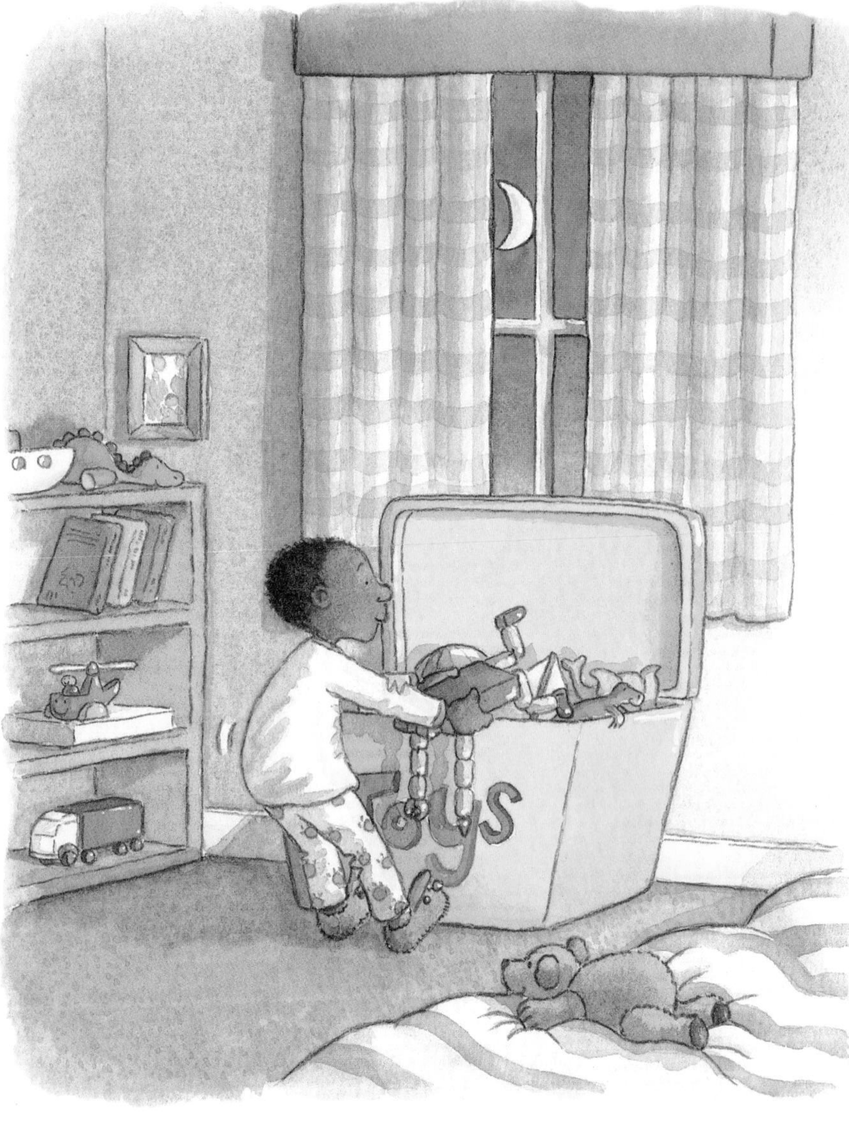

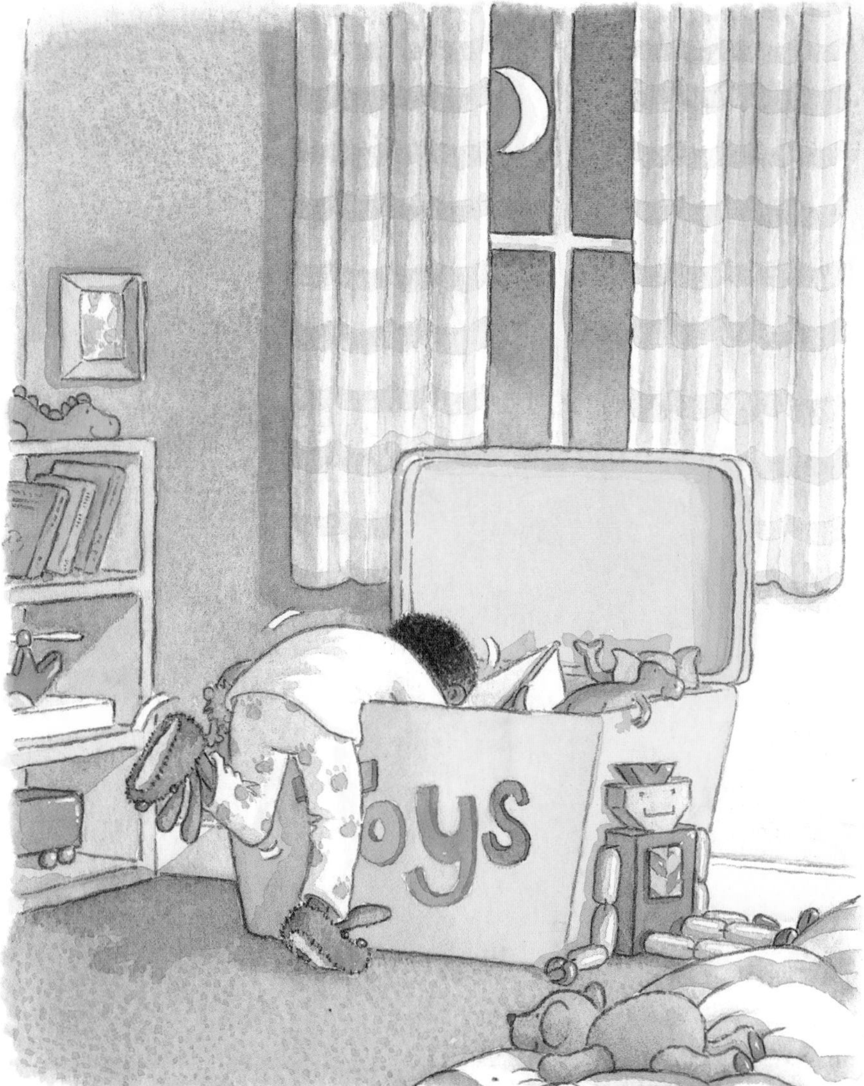
oys

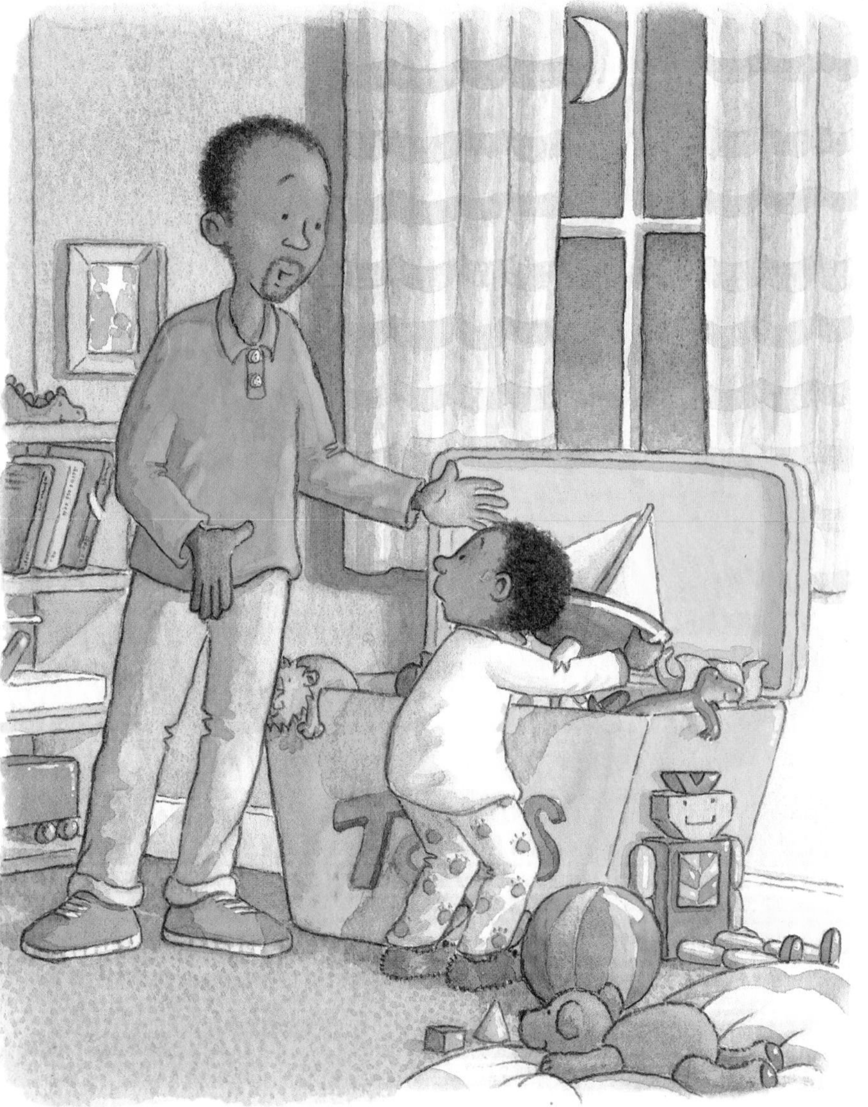

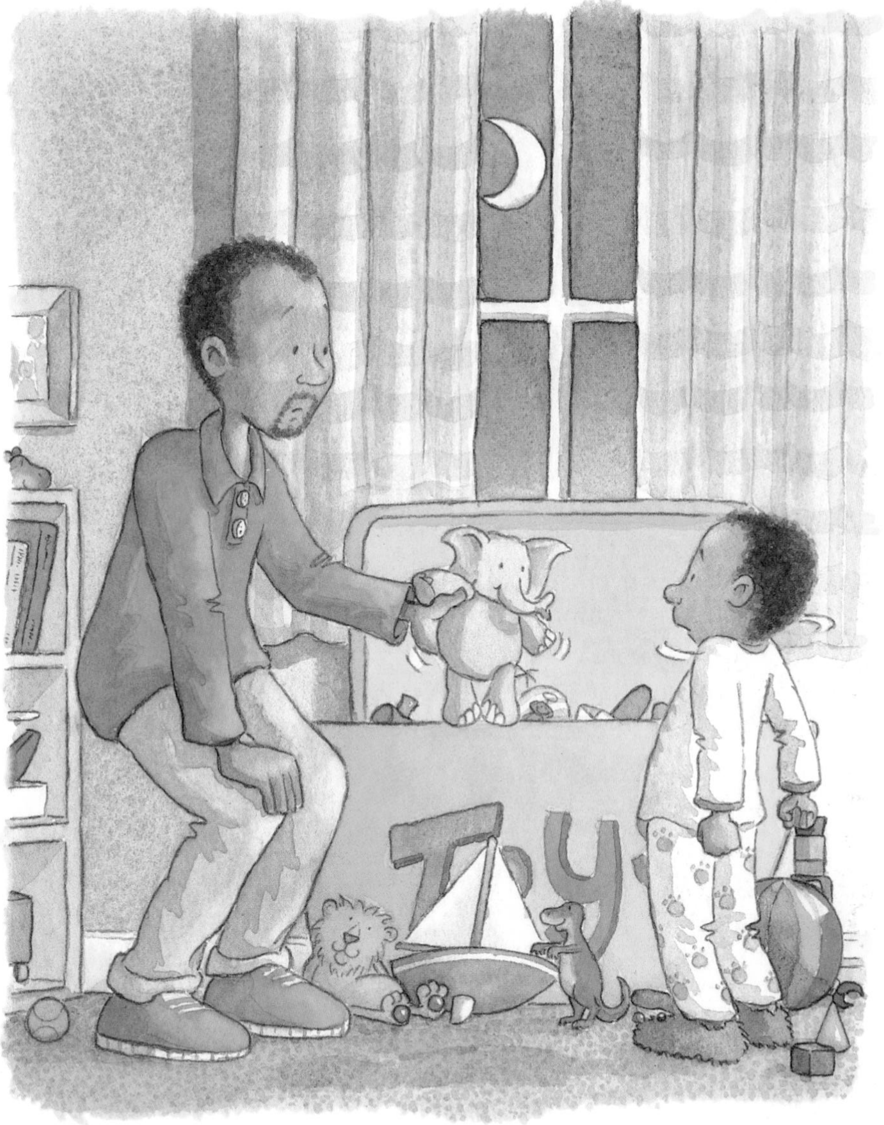

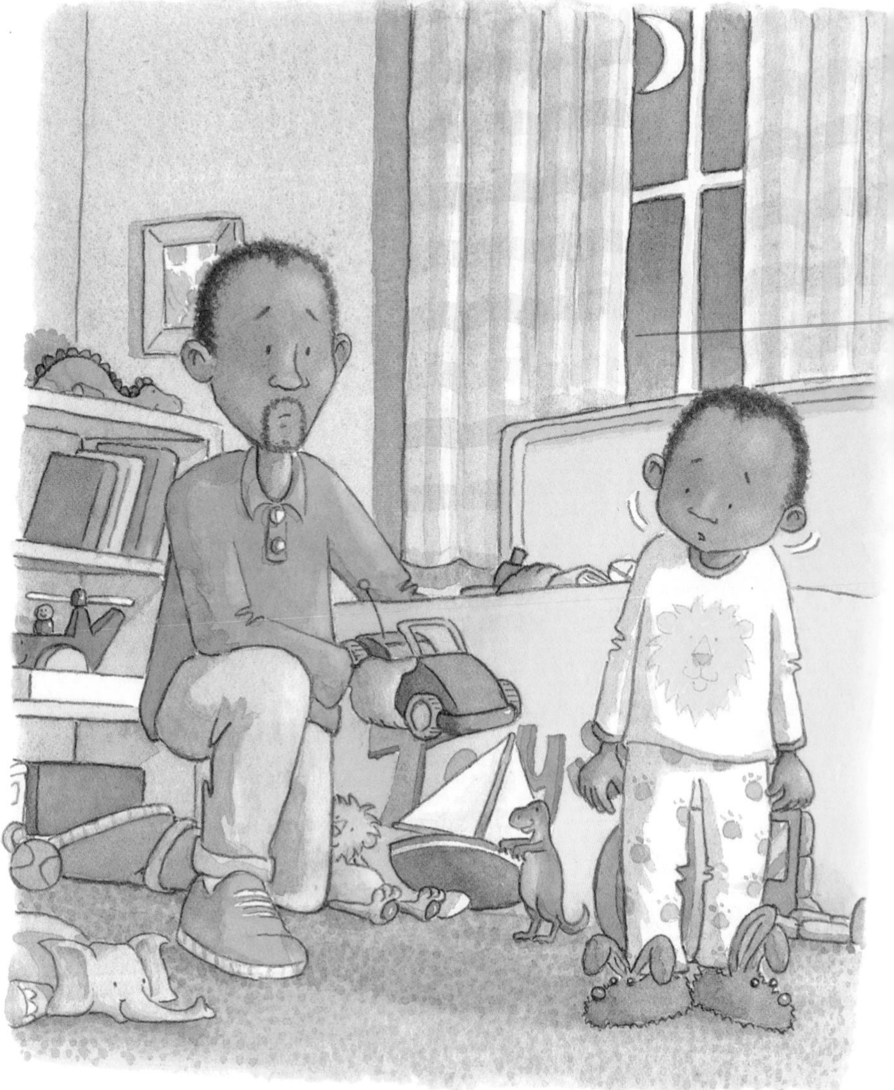

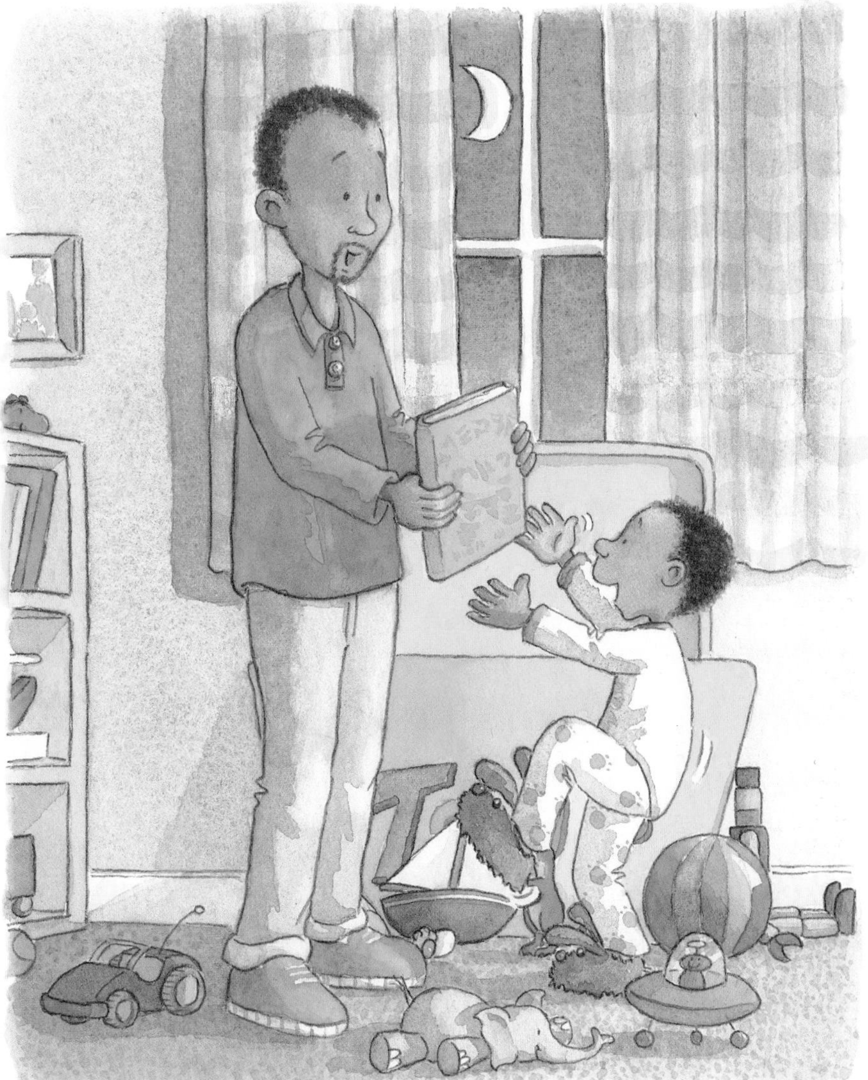

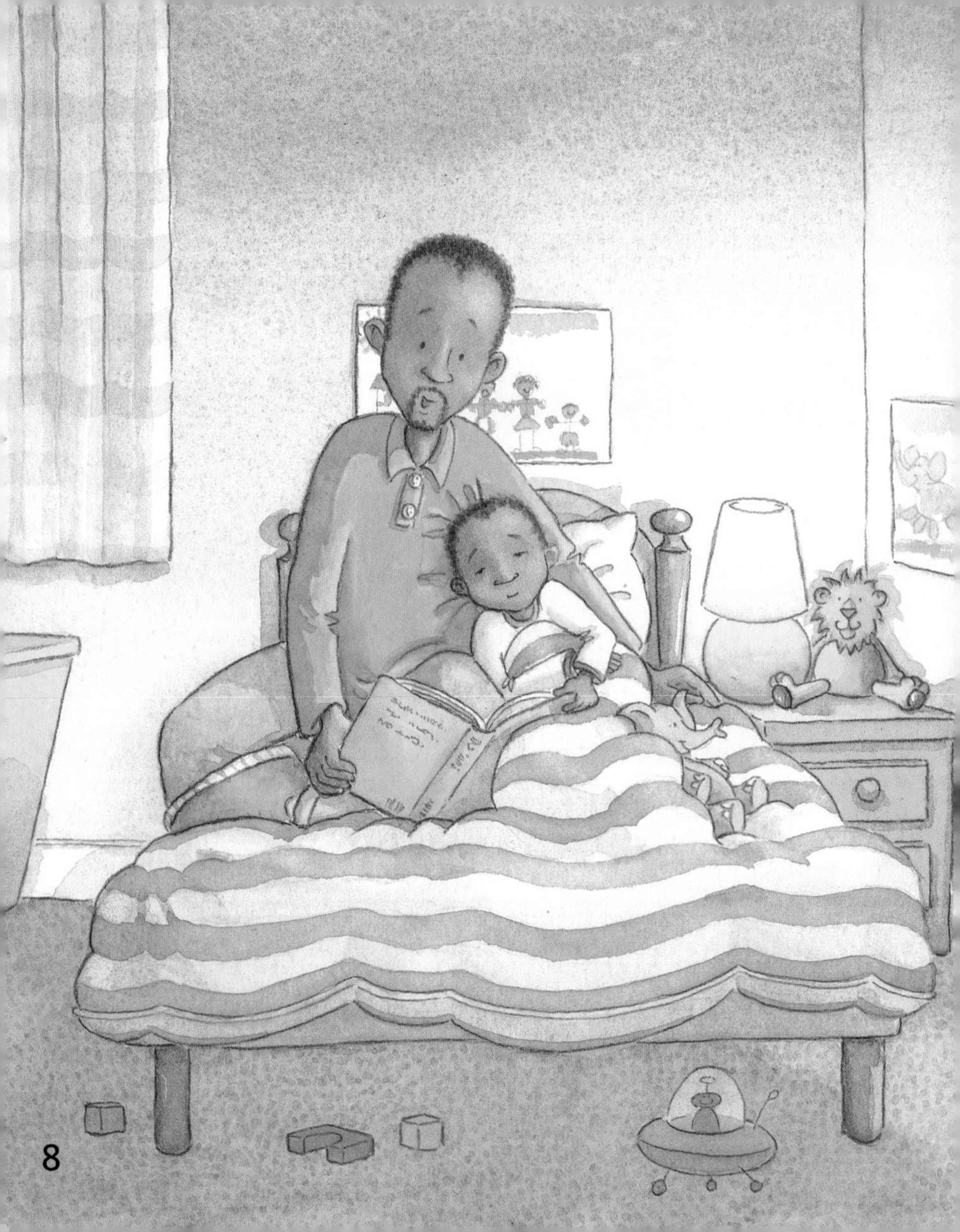